Bloomin' marvellous English from CGP

Pupils need to develop quite the repertoire of skills for Year 1 English... but have no fear! This cracking CGP book is simply bursting with practice.

It covers a huge range of topics from across the Year 1 curriculum, all packed into engaging activities. There's an exercise for every single day of spring term — wow!

And what's more, there are heaps of examples and colourful pictures to keep pupils interested. It's ideal for the classroom, home... wherever!

What CGP is all about

Our sole aim here at CGP is to produce the highest quality books
— carefully written, immaculately presented and
dangerously close to being funny.

Then we work our socks off to get them out to you
— at the cheapest possible prices.

Contents

☑ Use the tick boxes to help keep a record of which tests have been attempted.

Week 1
☐ Day 1 1
☐ Day 2 2
☐ Day 3 3
☐ Day 4 4
☐ Day 5 5

Week 2
☐ Day 1 6
☐ Day 2 7
☐ Day 3 8
☐ Day 4 9
☐ Day 5 10

Week 3
☐ Day 1 11
☐ Day 2 12
☐ Day 3 13
☐ Day 4 14
☐ Day 5 15

Week 4
☐ Day 1 16
☐ Day 2 17
☐ Day 3 18
☐ Day 4 19
☐ Day 5 20

Week 5
☐ Day 1 21
☐ Day 2 22
☐ Day 3 23
☐ Day 4 24
☐ Day 5 25

Week 6
☐ Day 1 26
☐ Day 2 27
☐ Day 3 28
☐ Day 4 29
☐ Day 5 30

Week 7
☐ Day 1 31
☐ Day 2 32
☐ Day 3 33
☐ Day 4 34
☐ Day 5 35

Week 8
☐ Day 1 36
☐ Day 2 37
☐ Day 3 38
☐ Day 4 39
☐ Day 5 40

Week 9
- ☑ Day 1 41
- ☑ Day 2 42
- ☑ Day 3 43
- ☑ Day 4 44
- ☑ Day 5 45

Week 10
- ☑ Day 1 46
- ☑ Day 2 47
- ☑ Day 3 48
- ☑ Day 4 49
- ☑ Day 5 50

Week 11
- ☑ Day 1 51
- ☑ Day 2 52
- ☑ Day 3 53
- ☑ Day 4 54
- ☑ Day 5 55

Week 12
- ☑ Day 1 56
- ☑ Day 2 57
- ☑ Day 3 58
- ☑ Day 4 59
- ☑ Day 5 60

Answers 61

Published by CGP

ISBN: 978 1 78908 676 8

Editors: Emma Cleasby, Alex Fairer, Rebecca Greaves, Catherine Heygate, Becca Lakin, Katya Parkes

With thanks to Claire Boulter and Juliette Green for the proofreading.

With thanks to Lottie Edwards for the copyright research.

Cover and Graphics used throughout the book © www.edu-clips.com

Printed by Bell & Bain Ltd, Glasgow.
Based on the classic CGP style created by Richard Parsons.

Text, design, layout and original illustrations © Coordination Group Publications Ltd. (CGP) 2020
All rights reserved.

Photocopying this book is not permitted, even if you have a CLA licence.
Extra copies are available from CGP with next day delivery • 0800 1712 712 • www.cgpbooks.co.uk

How to Use this Book

- This book contains 60 pages of daily English practice.
- We've split them into 12 sections — that's roughly one for each week of the Year 1 Spring term.
- Each week is made up of 5 pages, so there's one for every school day of the term (Monday – Friday).
- Each page should take about 10 minutes to complete.
- The pages contain a mix of topics from Year 1 English. New Year 1 topics are gradually introduced as you go through the book.
- The pages increase in difficulty as you progress through the book.
- Answers can be found at the back of the book.
- Each page looks something like this:

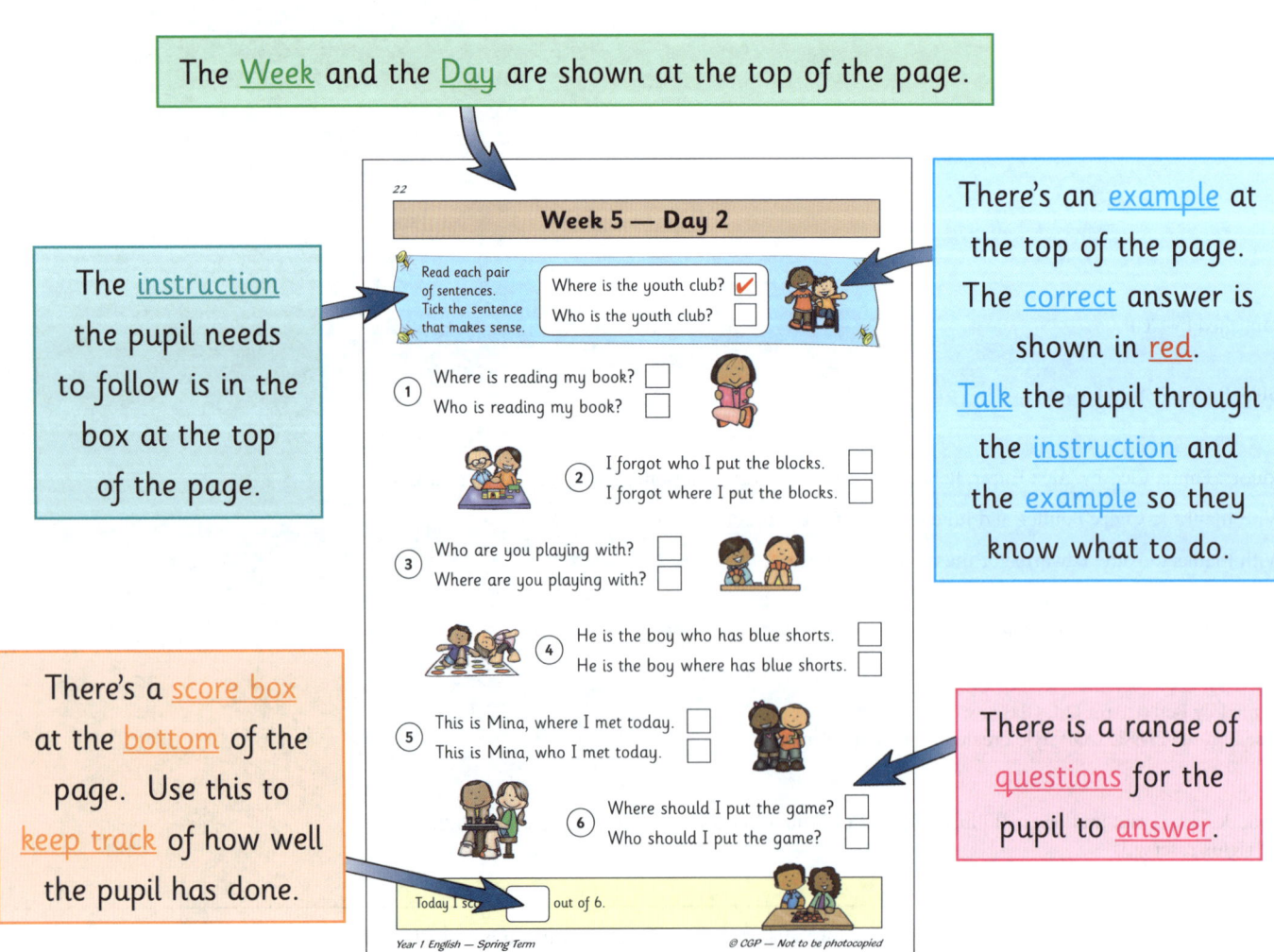

Week 1 — Day 1

Fill in the gap with either '**nk**' or '**ng**' to complete each word.

ha**ng**......

  swi..........

  pi..........

  wi..........

  tru..........

  dri..........

  si..........

  sti..........

 thi..........

Today I scored ☐ out of 8.

Week 1 — Day 2

Write the sentences below using spaces. Use the pictures to help you.

Wewenttothepark.

We went to the park.

1) Ifedtheducks.

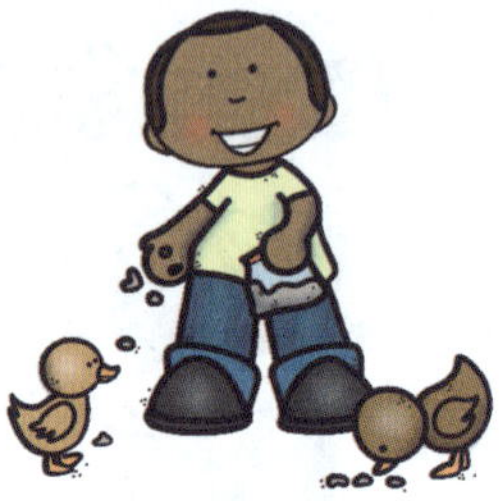

....

....

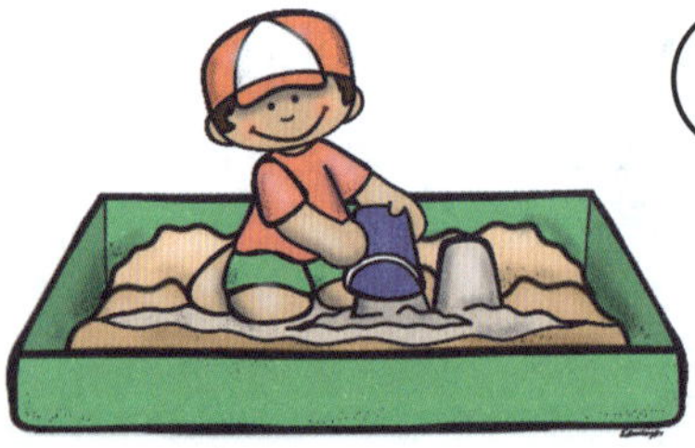

2) Lukeplayedinthesand.

....

....

3) Janehadalolly.

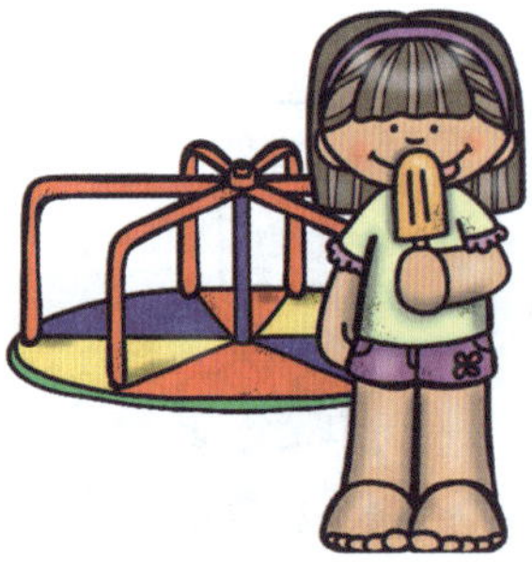

....

....

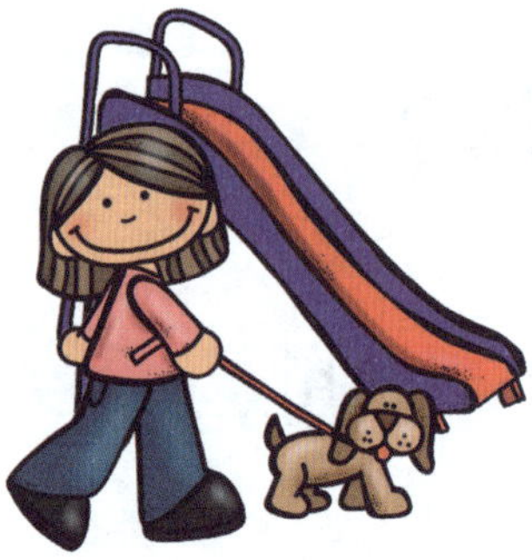

4) Isawabrowndog.

....

....

Today I scored ☐ out of 4.

Week 1 — Day 3

Circle 'yes' or 'no' to show whether each sentence uses '**and**' correctly.

The dress is pink and has a belt.  (yes) no

1. His shorts are green and mine are red.  yes no

2. Her skirt and is plain her top is spotty.  yes no

3. I need my hat and my scarf.  yes no

4. My socks have spots yours have and stripes.  yes no

5. Kim and Tim have the same coat.  yes no

Today I scored ☐ out of 5.

Week 1 — Day 4

Draw lines to join each sentence to the missing word.

I ____ in the bushes. — looked

(1) My brother is ____ Ted.

(2) He ____ us to play hide and seek.

asked

(3) Alfie ____ if he could go first.

(4) He ____ happy to play.

called

(5) I ____ Ted if he would hide with me.

(6) Alfie ____ out my name loudly.

looked

(7) Nia ____ in the long grass.

Today I scored ☐ out of 7.

Year 1 English — Spring Term

Week 1 — Day 5

Read each pair of sentences. Tick the sentence that matches each picture.

They are in the car. ✓
The car is blue. ☐

1. The boy is jumping from a swing. ☐
   The boy is playing on a swing. ☐

2. Their cat is black. ☐
   They do not like cats. ☐

3. Oh no! The dog looks sad. ☐
   The dog is sitting down. ☐

4. The house has a pink roof. ☐
   The front door is closed. ☐

5. Mrs Bell has a red coat. ☐
   Mrs Bell has brown boots. ☐

Today I scored ☐ out of 5.

Week 2 — Day 1

Read the words. Circle the word that doesn't rhyme.

fin | thin | (fine) | bin

1. wild | fill | hill | will

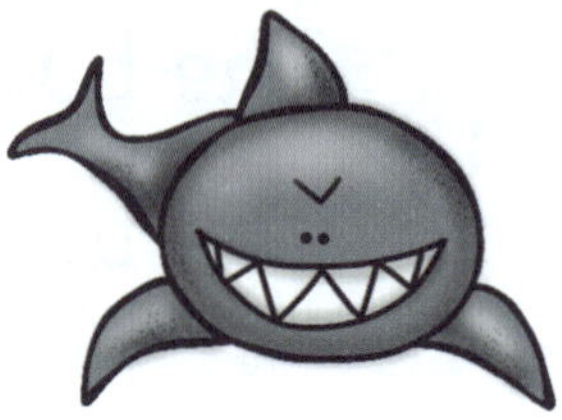

2. grin | win | kind | spin

3. bite | sit | hit | bit

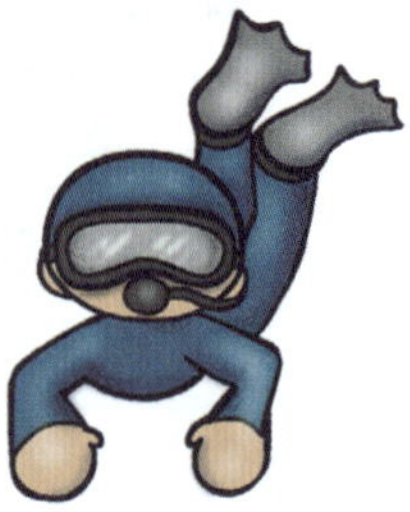

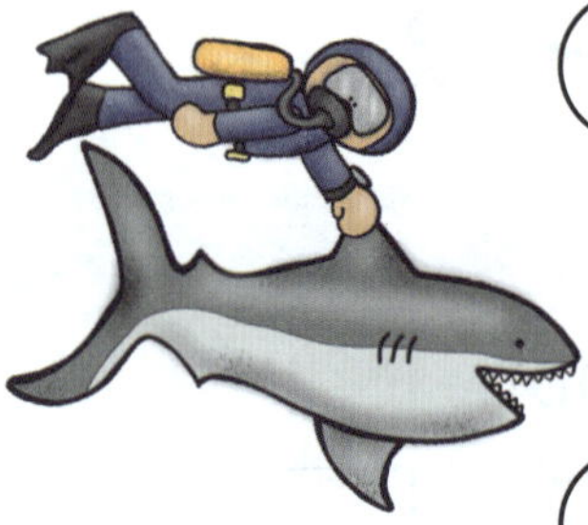

4. grip | tip | pipe | pip

5. ride | side | hide | grid

6. smile | mill | tile | pile

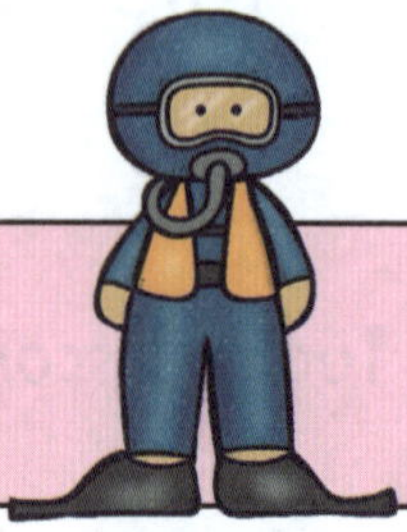

Today I scored ☐ out of 6.

Week 2 — Day 2

Read each sentence, then circle the correct spelling of the word in bold.

Cows eat **grass** / **gras**.

1. The **bul** / **bull** at the farm is brown.

 2. My dog is very **fluffy** / **flufy**.

3. The sheep are **blac** / **black**.

 4. I saw a bee **whizz** / **whiz** past.

5. A **duck** / **duk** is swimming in the pond.

 6. The snake **hised** / **hissed** at me.

Today I scored ☐ out of 6.

Week 2 — Day 3

Read each pair of sentences. Tick the sentence that uses capital letters correctly. In the last question, circle the four words that should have a capital letter.

I dance with Ryan. ✓
I dance with ryan. ☐

1. We see liam leaping through the air. ☐
   We see Liam leaping through the air. ☐

2. On Monday, I go to my dance lesson. ☐
   On Monday, i go to my dance lesson. ☐

3. Anita, Sam and Adam love music. ☐
   Anita, Sam and adam love music. ☐

4. My granny goes dancing on tuesday. ☐
   My granny goes dancing on Tuesday. ☐

5. Dear melissa,

   Will you come to the disco at school on friday?

   Holly and i will meet you there.

   From beth

Today I scored ☐ out of 8.

Week 2 — Day 4

Read each pair of sentences. Tick the sentence that uses full stops correctly.

He. wants to play ☐
He wants to play. ✓

1. We play cricket. ☐
   We. play. cricket. ☐

2. He. saved the goal ☐
   He saved the goal. ☐

3. They beat us. ☐
   They. beat us. ☐

4. I am the winner. ☐
   I am. the. winner ☐

5. Ben loves football. ☐
   Ben loves football ☐

6. I am good at tennis. ☐
   I am good at. tennis ☐

7. She is. the best player. ☐
   She is the best player. ☐

8. Pass the. ball to me. ☐
   Pass the ball to me. ☐

Today I scored ☐ out of 8.

Week 2 — Day 5

Look at the pictures. Use them to help you finish the sentences.

Henry

Henry is feeling worried.

Emily

Eli

Jack

Mirella

1) .... is giggling loudly.

2) .... is feeling cross.

3) .... is very upset.

4) .... is feeling pleased.

5) Draw a picture in the box to show how you are feeling.

Today I scored ☐ out of 5.

Week 3 — Day 1

Read each pair of sentences. Tick the sentence where the word in bold is spelled correctly.

Fech all the presents. ☐
Fetch all the presents. ✓

1. **Strech** to get it. ☐
   Stretch to get it. ☐

2. Pick **each** one up. ☐
   Pick **eatch** one up. ☐

3. It was in a **dich**. ☐
   It was in a **ditch**. ☐

4. These two **match**. ☐
   These two **mach**. ☐

5. **Croutch** to pick it up. ☐
   Crouch to pick it up. ☐

6. Do not **snatch** it. ☐
   Do not **snach** it. ☐

7. Look on the **bench**. ☐
   Look on the **bentch**. ☐

8. I had to **reatch** for it. ☐
   I had to **reach** for it. ☐

Today I scored ☐ out of 8.

Week 3 — Day 2

Draw lines to join each sentence to the missing word.

I have ____ my horse. — lost

1. Abby ____ her boots cleaned.

2. Ali ____ Zack how to make a fire.

3. She has to ____ on tight.

4. Sara found ____ in the river.

5. The hats ____ quickly.

6. The horse has brown ____.

7. Bill still has ____ found his cows.

told

got

sold

not

spots

hold

gold

Today I scored ☐ out of 7.

Week 3 — Day 3

Read each pair of sentences. Tick the sentence that uses capital letters correctly.

The starfish is little. ✓
the Starfish is little. ☐

1. jellyfish float in the Sea. ☐
   Jellyfish float in the sea. ☐

2. That fish has rainbow scales. ☐
   that fish has Rainbow scales. ☐

3. there Is a baby sea turtle. ☐
   There is a baby sea turtle. ☐

4. the seahorse is Bright yellow. ☐
   The seahorse is bright yellow. ☐

5. Octopuses can squirt ink. ☐
   octopuses can squirt Ink. ☐

6. A crab runs through the seaweed. ☐
   a Crab runs through the seaweed. ☐

Today I scored ☐ out of 6.

Week 3 — Day 4

Put the words in the right order to make a sentence.

Write either 1, 2, 3 or 4 in the boxes to show the order.

base	makes	Sue	the
4	2	1	3

1) likes   Nick   to   cook

2) toppings   the   gets   Olga

3) the   carries   plate   Molly

4) eat   starts   Jim   to

Today I scored ☐ out of 4.

Week 3 — Day 5

Read each sentence, then circle the picture that matches it.

Lots of different chickens live here.

1) It found a patch of grass.

4) A chicken is in the kitchen.

2) The hen sits on the nest.

5) A golden chick is hatching.

3) I have a chicken costume.

6) A chick stretches its wings.

 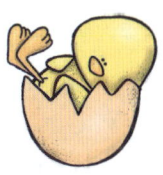

Today I scored ☐ out of 6.

Week 4 — Day 1

Read each sentence. Fill in the gap with either '**have**', '**said**' or '**so**'.

She went ..so.. fast.

1) Claire .... she felt very cold.

2) I would like to .... a hot drink.

3) Playing in the snow is .... much fun.

4) I .... got a green and yellow hat.

5) Mark .... he loves winter.

6) The ice over there is .... slippery.

7) They .... not finished making the snowman.

Today I scored ☐ out of 7.

Week 4 — Day 2

Read each word, then colour the picture that matches it.   broccoli

1. rice

2. carrot

3. picnic

4. ice

5. cake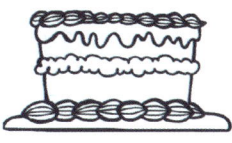

6. slice

7. cookie

8. cereal

Today I scored [ ] out of 8.

Week 4 — Day 3

Look at each picture, then circle the word that matches it.

1.  witch / witches

5.  sock / socks

2.  cat / cats

6.  frog / frogs

3.  dress / dresses

7.  broom / brooms

4.  book / books

8.  spider / spiders

Today I scored ☐ out of 8.

Year 1 English — Spring Term

Week 4 — Day 4

Read each sentence. Underline the word that should have a capital letter.

We are in <u>london</u>.

1) We moved to scotland three years ago.

2) Greg went to italy with his family.

3) Rose and mike live in England with their parents.

4) He is from Perth and i am from Cardiff.

5) Rich and Ava went to paris in August.

6) Jamie is going to Germany on thursday.

7) Fran and megan are going surfing in Cornwall.

Today I scored ☐ out of 7.

Week 4 — Day 5

Draw a line to match each pair of sentences to the correct picture.

I am made from wood.
You can keep books on me.

1. I show what time it is.
   I have numbers on me.

2. I have a handle.
   You can drink from me.

3. I have a long tail.
   I like to chase mice.

4. You can sit on me.
   I am covered in dots.

5. You can make a fire in me.
   I am made from stone.

Today I scored ☐ out of 5.

Week 5 — Day 1

Read each sentence. Fill in the gap with either '**what**' or '**when**'.

...**What**... a big puddle this is!

1) I saw Ewan .... I was playing outside.

2) Tia put her coat on .... it started to rain.

 3) Look at .... my dog is doing!

4) Yusif likes it .... it rains.

5) .... is that splashing sound?

6) .... will it be sunny again?

 7) She asked .... my dog is called.

8) .... a bright umbrella she has!

Today I scored ☐ out of 8.

Week 5 — Day 2

Read each pair of sentences. Tick the sentence that makes sense.

Where is the youth club? ✓
Who is the youth club? ☐

1) Where is reading my book? ☐
Who is reading my book? ☐

2) I forgot who I put the blocks. ☐
I forgot where I put the blocks. ☐

3) Who are you playing with? ☐
Where are you playing with? ☐

4) He is the boy who has blue shorts. ☐
He is the boy where has blue shorts. ☐

5) This is Mina, where I met today. ☐
This is Mina, who I met today. ☐

6) Where should I put the game? ☐
Who should I put the game? ☐

Today I scored ☐ out of 6.

Year 1 English — Spring Term

Week 5 — Day 3

Circle '?' or '.' to show whether each sentence should end with a question mark or a full stop.

Who is that (?) .

1) Do they have robes on ? .

2) He has leaves in his hair ? .

3) What is he holding ? .

4) It is a very hot day ? .

5) Where is that big boat going ? .

6) What is that statue made from ? .

7) He is holding a torch ? .

Today I scored [ ] out of 7.

Week 5 — Day 4

Read the sentences, then find the words in bold in the wordsearch. Circle the words when you find them.

1) Kings have **gold** crowns.

4) He has a **large** horse.

2) The castle is **grey**.

5) The **green** frog is happy.

3) The **giant** is smiling.

6) She has **magic** beans.

E	L	G	R	E	E	N	O	A	G	I	M
Y	B	O	I	G	S	L	D	U	R	B	A
E	U	L	L	A	R	G	E	O	E	N	G
G	I	A	N	T	O	G	R	I	Y	A	I
M	A	T	S	E	G	O	L	D	O	N	C

Today I scored ☐ out of 6.

Year 1 English — Spring Term

Week 5 — Day 5

Draw lines to match each question to the correct answer.

How old are you? —— I am six.

1. What is your name?  I live on Park Road.

2. Where do you live?  I am called Roger.

3. Who do you live with?  I love swimming.

4. What are your hobbies?  I have one goat.

5. Do you have any pets?  I live with my mum and my little sister.

Today I scored ☐ out of 5.

Week 6 — Day 1

Add 's' or 'es' to the word in bold to complete each sentence.

Noah **run**s.... home.

1) Dev **walk**.......... to the park.

2) Zoe **whizz**.......... past us.

3) The bus **splash**.......... through the rain.

4) We left our **lunch**.......... in the car.

5) Lucy and I rode our **scooter**..........

6) She **catch**.......... the train.

7) My dad **drive**.......... to work.

8) We go to school on our **bike**..........

Today I scored ☐ out of 8.

Week 6 — Day 2

Read each sentence. Circle 'yes' or 'no' to show whether the letters '**ow**' make the same sound in the words in bold.

The **owl** is by the **tower**.

yes   no

1) I let her **borrow** my **pillow**.    yes   no

2) The **yellow** owl is waving **now**.    yes   no

3) The **brown** owl has a **crown**.    yes   no

4) He is **below** the **rainbow**.    yes   no

5) She has **grown** a **flower**.    yes   no

6) They **show** us **how** to spell.    yes   no

Today I scored ☐ out of 6.

Week 6 — Day 3

Read each pair of sentences. Tick the sentence that could end with an exclamation mark.

It is so sour ✓
Do you like it ☐

1. I eat so much fruit ☐
   Do you eat fruit ☐

2. Is that yummy ☐
   How yummy this is ☐

3. Where is my lemon ☐
   I lost my lemon ☐

4. The fruit can talk ☐
   What did it say ☐

5. How big is the melon ☐
   That melon is huge ☐

6. The peach has eyes ☐
   Is it looking at me ☐

7. What a strange apple ☐
   Why is it so cross ☐

8. Can I have a banana ☐
   Bananas are so nice ☐

Today I scored ☐ out of 8.

Week 6 — Day 4

Read each sentence. Fill in the gap with either '**little**' or '**one**'.

He dug ...**one**... hole.

1) My .... brother likes the sand.

2) I found .... crab.

3) We have .... beach ball.

4) Emma put a .... flag on top.

5) The pink .... is mine.

6) I saw some .... fish.

7) There is .... chair left.

Today I scored ☐ out of 7.

Week 6 — Day 5

Read the sentences, then answer the questions.

Becky and her little sister like to dress up as princesses. Becky has a crown with green and purple gems.

1) Circle the picture that shows the hat Becky owns.

Becky pretends to fight dragons with a bow and arrow.

2) What does Becky pretend to fight dragons with?

....

They make a castle out of boxes. It has a small tower and a yellow flag.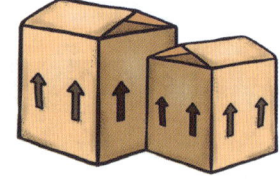

3) Draw a picture of the castle.

Today I scored ☐ out of 4.

Year 1 English — Spring Term © CGP — Not to be photocopied

Week 7 — Day 1

Circle 'yes' or 'no' to show whether the sentence matches the picture.

Dad cooked a chicken.  yes no

1) Jake is eating a sandwich.  yes no

2) Nadia loves school dinners.  yes no

3) I have chips for lunch.  yes no

4) The chef has a white hat.  yes no

5) She holds a bunch of grapes.  yes no

6) It made my stomach ache.  yes no

7) I chew with my mouth open.  yes no

Today I scored ☐ out of 7.

Week 7 — Day 2

Read each sentence. Circle the correct ending to complete the word in bold.

I **bang**__ the drum.   ing   (ed)

1. We **listen**__ to the music.   ing   ed

2. Nasim wants to be a **sing**__.   ing   er

3. She loves **learn**__ the keyboard.   ing   ed

4. He is our music **teach**__.   er   ed

5. They **start**__ to sing.   ed   ing

6. **Play**__ the flute is such fun.   ing   er

7. Are you **go**__ to the show?   er   ing

8. Ruby **clean**__ her trumpet.   ed   er

Today I scored ☐ out of 8.

Week 7 — Day 3

Read each sentence. Underline the word that should start with a capital letter. Then add a full stop to the sentence.

<u>i</u> have two puppies.

(1) Their names are rory and Daisy

(2) my sister Anna says the puppies are clever

(3) Anna and i saw Rory juggling five balls

(4) I showed daisy how to read

(5) My brother joe took the puppies on a plane

(6) now they want to learn how to fly

Today I scored [ ] out of 12.

Week 7 — Day 4

Read each pair of words. Circle the word that matches the picture.

 happy **(unhappy)**

1.  tied / untied

2.  sure / unsure

3.  helpful / unhelpful

4.  kind / unkind

5.  caring / uncaring

6.  steady / unsteady

7.  pack / unpack

8.  afraid / unafraid

Today I scored ☐ out of 8.

Week 7 — Day 5

Use the picture to help you answer the questions below.

1) Who is painting? ....

2) Who is sitting on a yellow chair? ....

> Mrs Sims asked the class to tidy up before lunch.

3) What is the teacher called? ....

> Sam looked at his desk and felt sad. It was so untidy! Amy and Mia stayed and helped Sam with the tidying.

4) What did Mia and Amy help Sam do? Tick one box.

eat his lunch ☐   tidy his desk ☐   check his bag ☐

Today I scored ☐ out of 4.

© CGP — Not to be photocopied

Year 1 English — Spring Term

Week 8 — Day 1

Draw lines to join each sentence to the missing word.

We love going to visit our ___. — aunties

1. Auntie Evie lets us splash around in our ___.

cries

2. Auntie Ellie ___ at films.

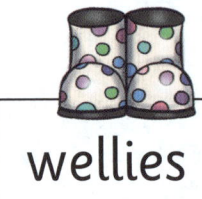

wellies

3. Auntie Rosie reads me ___.

strawberries

4. Auntie Amie loves ___ eggs.

jellies

5. I help Auntie Jennie make ___.

stories

6. Auntie Zadie grows ___.

fried

Today I scored ☐ out of 6.

Week 8 — Day 2

Read each sentence. Fill in the gap with either '**do**' or '**out**'.

I ..do.. the washing.

1) I help my dad .... the **c**ooking.

2) Archie sorts .... the clot**h**es.

3) My older brother can .... the ir**o**ning.

4) Milo and Dad go .... with the dog eve**r**y day.

5) Mum and I .... som**e** dusting.

6) She put**s** the rubbish ....

7) The green letters spell out a word. Write the word to complete the sentence.

We help with the ....

Today I scored ☐ out of 7.

Week 8 — Day 3

Circle '.' or '?' to show whether each sentence should end with a full stop or a question mark.

Will you play with me
. **?**

1) Is that your kite
   . ?

2) They are friends
   . ?

3) What do you eat
   . ?

4) Why are you pink
   . ?

5) I like those flowers
   . ?

6) Where is your hat
   . ?

7) He has yellow boots
   . ?

8) She looks cosy
   . ?

Today I scored ☐ out of 8.

Week 8 — Day 4

Tick the box where '**and**' should go in each sentence.

This morning, we ☐ did English ✓ PE.

1) Avni has a pencil ☐ I have ☐ a pen.

2) I ☐ like maths ☐ you like science.

3) Max ☐ Leni love ☐ school.

4) My bag ☐ is blue ☐ green.

5) Our teacher ☐ is kind ☐ funny.

6) We line up ☐ wait for ☐ lunch.

7) He is ☐ painting ☐ she is reading.

8) Ella ☐ carries the paper ☐ the glue.

Today I scored ☐ out of 8.

Week 8 — Day 5

Read the sentences below, then answer the questions.

Auntie Susan works as a baker in a shop.

① Circle the picture that shows Auntie Susan.

Auntie Susan makes all sorts of yummy things, like brownies, cookies and cakes.

② What does Auntie Susan make? Tick two things.

brownies ☐   muffins ☐   cookies ☐

Last week, Auntie Susan made a pie filled with cherries and blackberries. It was the nicest pie I have ever tried.

③ What was in Auntie Susan's pie? Write down two things.

....

Today I scored ☐ out of 5.

Week 9 — Day 1

Draw lines to match each sentence to the correct picture.

Please can we have a picnic?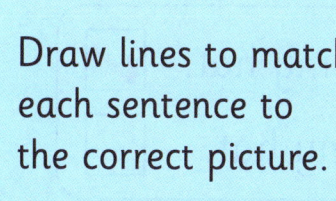

(1) This peach looks so tasty.

(2) She eats ice cream at the beach.

(3) I spread the jam on the bread.

(4) We have one bag of crisps each.

(5) I dream about snack time.

(6) I got a jar of peanut butter.

(7) Carrots are very healthy.

Today I scored ☐ out of 7.

Week 9 — Day 2

Read each pair of sentences. Tick the sentence that is spelt correctly.

Give me my hat. ✓
Giv me my hat. ☐

1. I driv to the house. ☐
   I drive to the house. ☐

2. He is very brave. ☐
   He is very brafe. ☐

3. They arrive in time. ☐
   They arrivve in time. ☐

4. Please saev my cat. ☐
   Please save my cat. ☐

5. I wave at her. ☐
   I waiv at her. ☐

6. We wear thick gloves. ☐
   We wear thick glovs. ☐

7. I leafe when it is over. ☐
   I leave when it is over. ☐

8. He is above me. ☐
   He is abov me. ☐

Today I scored ☐ out of 8.

Week 9 — Day 3

Put the words in the right order to make a sentence.
Write either 1, 2, 3 or 4 in the boxes to show the order.

| three | see | I | bats |
| 3 | 2 | 1 | 4 |

1) looks   after   Ivan   bats

2) finds   bats   Jay   some

3) caves   Tanya   the   visits

4) Ruth   up   dressing   likes

5) bats   chase   Pablo   the

Today I scored ☐ out of 5.

Week 9 — Day 4

Read each pair of sentences. Tick the sentence that uses capital letters correctly.

I have brown hair. ✓
i have brown hair. ☐

1. jen has a pink hair clip. ☐
   Jen has a pink hair clip. ☐

2. Santino and i like to smile. ☐
   Santino and I like to smile. ☐

3. my hair is long and curly. ☐
   My hair is long and curly. ☐

4. Lia looks a lot like Tess. ☐
   Lia looks a lot like tess. ☐

5. He has a light blue shirt. ☐
   he has a light blue shirt. ☐

6. ally wears a gold necklace. ☐
   Ally wears a gold necklace. ☐

7. Yusra is taller than i am. ☐
   Yusra is taller than I am. ☐

Today I scored ☐ out of 7.

Week 9 — Day 5

Read the sentences below, then answer the questions.

> Surfing is lots of fun. You can stand on top of a surfboard and ride waves back to the beach.

1) What do you stand on when you are surfing?

....

> You can take surfing lessons at the beach. Your teacher will give you lots of help when you are learning to surf.

2) Where can you learn how to surf?

in the desert ☐   at a lake ☐   at the beach ☐

3) Some people paint their surfboards. Colour in this picture to show how you would paint your own surfboard.

Today I scored ☐ out of 3.

Week 10 — Day 1

Read each sentence. Fill in the gap with either 'come', 'like' or 'some'.

I ..*like*.. packing my case.

1) Milly put .... sunglasses in her bag.

2) Luca would .... to bring his book.

3) My teddy will .... with me.

4) We need .... towels.

5) I .... to take crayons with me.

6) We will pack .... socks.

7) Please can you .... and help me carry it?

Today I scored ☐ out of 7.

Week 10 — Day 2

Read each sentence. Write the correct name under each picture.

Rob is a cleaner.

Rob

Kath wants to be an author.

Tom serves food and drink.

Nico is training to be a dancer.

Hans is a bus driver.

Ian delivers letters and parcels.

1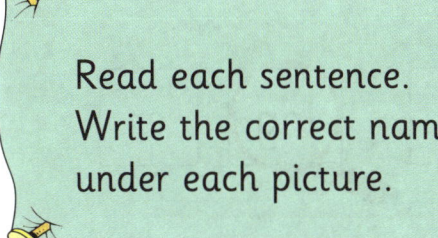

2

3

4

5

Today I scored ☐ out of 5.

Week 10 — Day 3

Read each sentence. Circle the correct ending to complete the word in bold.

My class likes **act**__. | (ing) | er |

1) Oliver **walk**__ onto the stage. | ed | er |

2) **Read**__ lines is really fun. | er | ing |

3) Andy **play**__ a cheeky puppy. | er | ed |

4) Ling **turn**__ up on time. | ing | ed |

5) Alba is the loudest **speak**__. | ing | er |

6) Ron **miss**__ the show. | ed | ing |

7) My friends are very good at **sing**__. | er | ing |

8) Bella **dress**__ as a cat. | ed | er |

Today I scored ☐ out of 8.

Week 10 — Day 4

Read each pair of sentences. Tick the sentence that uses the correct punctuation mark.

Oh no, I am lost! ✓
Oh no, I am lost? ☐

1. Where can I get a map? ☐
Where can I get a map! ☐

2. Thank you for helping me! ☐
Thank you for helping me? ☐

3. Should I turn left or right! ☐
Should I turn left or right? ☐

4. Which way is the fastest! ☐
Which way is the fastest? ☐

5. That was such a long road! ☐
That was such a long road? ☐

6. I have found the zoo at last? ☐
I have found the zoo at last! ☐

Today I scored ☐ out of 6.

Week 10 — Day 5

Read the sentences below, then answer the questions.

Mrs Turner lives in a house made of gingerbread. She has a silver cat named Berty who likes treats.

1 Circle the house that Mrs Turner lives in.

2 What kind of animal is Berty?

....

Mrs Turner is a **kind** person. She gives Berty treats, but he has to eat every bit of his dinner first.

3 Which word means the same as '**kind**'?

nervous ☐   nice ☐   strict ☐

4 How can Berty make sure he gets treats?

....

Today I scored ☐ out of 4.

Year 1 English — Spring Term

Week 11 — Day 1

Read each sentence. Fill in the gap with either '**were**' or '**there**'.

Dad said ...there... was snow.

1) We .... ready to make a snowman.

2) My friend Peter was .... too.

3) Our snowmen .... so big.

4) Look at that one over ....!

5) Are .... any carrots left?

6) The arms .... made from sticks.

7) .... are the buttons we used for eyes.

8) I thought they .... never going to melt.

Today I scored ☐ out of 8.

Week 11 — Day 2

Read each sentence. Circle 'yes' or 'no' to show whether the sentence matches the picture.

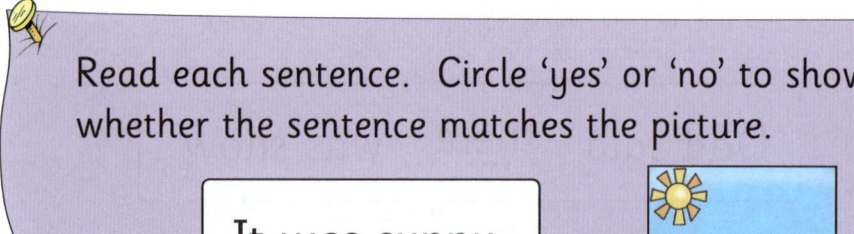

It was sunny. — **yes** / no

1) I wanted to run around.  yes / no

2) There was grass by the path.  yes / no

3) I passed through a field.  yes / no

4) I put flowers in my basket.  yes / no

5) A wasp was on the petal.  yes / no

6) I made a flower headband.  yes / no

Today I scored ☐ out of 6.

Week 11 — Day 3

Draw lines to join each sentence to the missing word.

I could see the ____ castle. —— bouncy

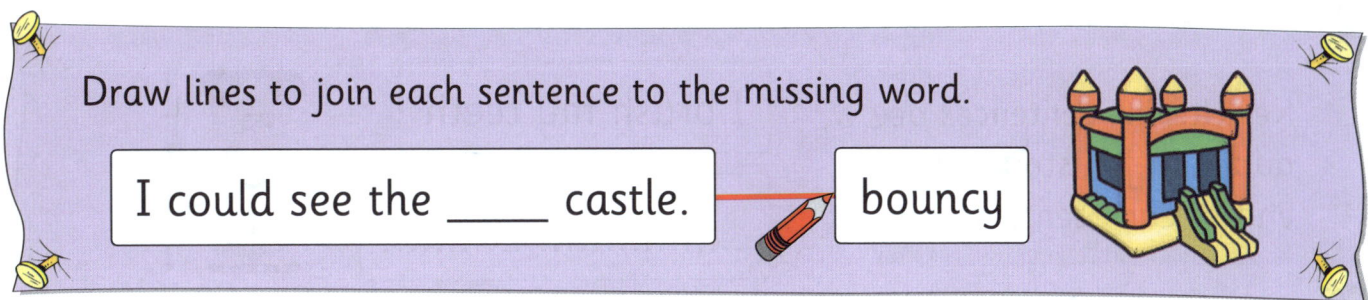

1) My little ____ Leo came with me.

you

2) Can ____ jump high?

cousin

3) A ____ of children joined in with us.

counted

4) We ____ touch the top.

around

5) I ____ how many times I jumped.

group

6) My ____ were hurting.

could

7) We ran ____ to the slide.

shoulders

Today I scored ☐ out of 7.

Week 11 — Day 4

Rewrite the sentences below, adding a full stop to the end of each sentence.

I brush my teeth

..I brush my teeth..

1) Robert smiles very widely

....

2) Elsa has two toothbrushes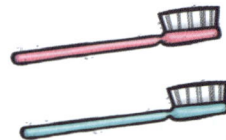

....

3) Marco is a dentist

....

4) Penny lost her tooth

....

Today I scored ☐ out of 4.

Week 11 — Day 5

The sentences below are part of a poem.
Read the sentences, then answer the questions.

As Annie looked up at a dark rain **clowd**,
She heard a great rumble that was very loud.

(1) Write the correct spelling of the word in bold.

clowd ....

She panicked and dropped her drink with a splash,
Then waited for the next bolt of lightning to flash.

(2) What does Annie think made the rumbling noise?

a lorry ☐   an animal ☐   a storm ☐

Her brother Taj laughed as she looked around.
It was his tummy that had made the sound!

(3) What really made the rumbling noise? Circle one thing.

| Taj's tummy | a plane | the rain clouds |

Today I scored ☐ out of 3.

Week 12 — Day 1

Draw lines to join each sentence to the missing word.

We visited the castle in ____. — July

1) My ____ were excited to see the castle.

2) We waited ____ the gate.

3) You had to show ____ ticket.

4) It was ____ busy inside.

5) There were ____ things to see.

6) I bought ____ a gift from the shop.

7) I am glad the weather was ____.

many

dry

by

myself

family

very

your

Today I scored ☐ out of 7.

Week 12 — Day 2

Read each sentence. Fill in the gap with either '**little**', '**one**', '**do**' or '**out**'.

We wanted to ..do.. something fun.

1) We went .... to look for butterflies.

2) Jerry saw a pink .... by the tree.

3) There were some .... butterflies in the field.

4) .... landed on my head.

5) It had .... stripes on its wings.

6) I asked Jerry what I should ....

7) I helped it get .... of my hair.

8) .... you like butterflies?

Today I scored [ ] out of 8.

Week 12 — Day 3

Look at the pictures, then read the sentences. Write the numbers 1 to 5 in the boxes to put the sentences in the right order.

I love ice cream. 1

1) Mum came back with a huge ice cream. ☐

2) I was very upset and nearly cried. ☐

3) Oh no! I dropped it on the ground! ☐

4) Mum went to buy me a yummy treat. ☐

5) I sat on a bench and waited for her. ☐

Today I scored ☐ out of 5.

Week 12 — Day 4

Read each sentence. Fill in the gap with either '**what**' or '**when**'.

<u>When</u> will we arrive at the hotel?

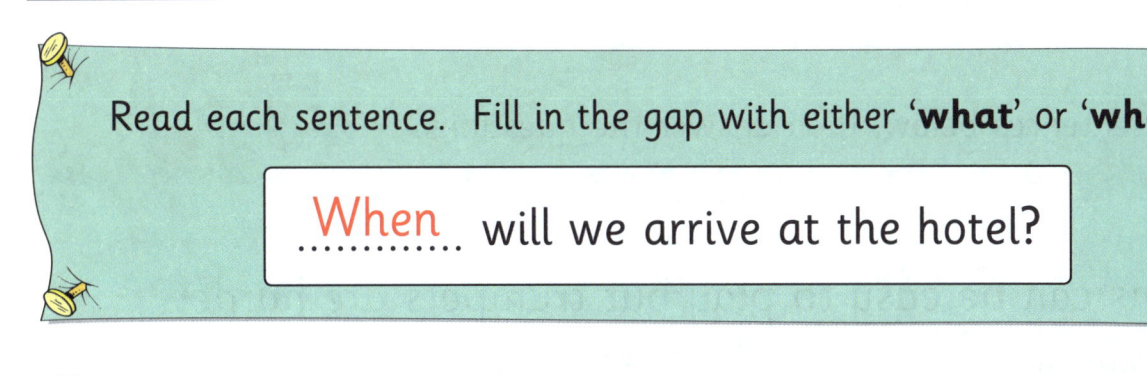

1) .... will our room be ready?

2) .... floor is our room on?

3) .... is our room number?

4) .... is breakfast served?

5) .... do the shops open?

6) .... is on the dinner menu?

7) .... has the weather been like?

8) .... do we have to leave the hotel?

Today I scored ☐ out of 8.

Week 12 — Day 5

Read the sentences below, then answer the questions.

> Drums can be easy to play but trumpets are harder.
> You use your mouth and fingers to play a trumpet.
> You can use a stick or your hands to play a drum.

1) Circle the musical instrument that can be easy to play.

2) What can you use to play a drum? Tick one box.

handle ☐   mouth ☐   stick ☐

> A harp is a type of instrument. Harps normally have a wooden frame. You pluck the strings to make a sound.

3) What is the frame of a harp normally made from?

....

4) What do you think people use to play a harp?

ball ☐   mouth ☐   fingers ☐

Today I scored ☐ out of 4.

Answers

Week 1 — Day 1
1. swi**ng**
2. wi**ng**
3. dri**nk**
4. sti**ng**
5. pi**nk**
6. tru**nk**
7. si**ng**
8. thi**nk**

Week 1 — Day 2
1. I fed the ducks.
2. Luke played in the sand.
3. Jane had a lolly.
4. I saw a brown dog.

Week 1 — Day 3
1. yes
2. no
3. yes
4. no
5. yes

Week 1 — Day 4
1. My brother is **called** Ted.
2. He **asked** us to play hide and seek.
3. Alfie **asked** if he could go first.
4. He **looked** happy to play.
5. I **asked** Ted if he would hide with me.
6. Alfie **called** out my name loudly.
7. Nia **looked** in the long grass.

Week 1 — Day 5
1. The boy is playing on a swing.
2. Their cat is black.
3. The dog is sitting down.
4. The front door is closed.
5. Mrs Bell has brown boots.

Week 2 — Day 1
1. wild
2. kind
3. bite
4. pipe
5. grid
6. mill

Week 2 — Day 2
1. The **bull** at the farm is brown.
2. My dog is very **fluffy**.
3. The sheep are **black**.
4. I saw a bee **whizz** past.
5. A **duck** is swimming in the pond.
6. The snake **hissed** at me.

Week 2 — Day 3
1. We see Liam leaping through the air.
2. On Monday, I go to my dance lesson.
3. Anita, Sam and Adam love music.
4. My granny goes dancing on Tuesday.
5.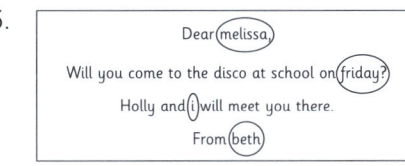

Week 2 — Day 4
1. We play cricket.
2. He saved the goal.
3. They beat us.
4. I am the winner.
5. Ben loves football.
6. I am good at tennis.
7. She is the best player.
8. Pass the ball to me.

Week 2 — Day 5
1. **Mirella** is giggling loudly.
2. **Emily** is feeling cross.
3. **Eli** is very upset.
4. **Jack** is feeling pleased.
5. Any sensible drawing.

Week 3 — Day 1
1. **Stretch** to get it.
2. Pick **each** one up.
3. It was in a **ditch**.
4. These two **match**.
5. **Crouch** to pick it up.
6. Do not **snatch** it.
7. Look on the **bench**.
8. I had to **reach** for it.

Week 3 — Day 2
1. Abby **got** her boots cleaned.
2. Ali **told** Zack how to make a fire.
3. She has to **hold** on tight.
4. Sara found **gold** in the river.
5. The hats **sold** quickly.
6. The horse has brown **spots**.
7. Bill still has **not** found his cows.

Week 3 — Day 3
1. Jellyfish float in the sea.
2. That fish has rainbow scales.
3. There is a baby sea turtle.
4. The seahorse is bright yellow.
5. Octopuses can squirt ink.
6. A crab runs through the seaweed.

Week 3 — Day 4
1. likes Nick to cook

   | 2 | 1 | 3 | 4 |

2. toppings the gets Olga

   | 4 | 3 | 2 | 1 |

3. the carries plate Molly

   | 3 | 2 | 4 | 1 |

4. eat starts Jim to

   | 4 | 2 | 1 | 3 |

Week 3 — Day 5

1.
4.
2.
5.
3.
6.

Week 4 — Day 1

1. Claire **said** she felt very cold.
2. I would like to **have** a hot drink.
3. Playing in the snow is **so** much fun.
4. I **have** got a green and yellow hat.
5. Mark **said** he loves winter.
6. The ice over there is **so** slippery.
7. They **have** not finished making the snowman.

Week 4 — Day 2

1.
2.
3.
4.
5.
6.
7.
8.

(with pictures: 1. rice, 2. carrot, 3. basket, 4. ice, 5. cake, 6. pie, 7. cookie, 8. fish)

Week 4 — Day 3

1. witches
2. cat
3. dresses
4. book
5. socks
6. frogs
7. broom
8. spiders

Week 4 — Day 4

1. We moved to <u>scotland</u> three years ago.
2. Greg went to <u>italy</u> with his family.
3. Rose and <u>mike</u> live in England with their parents.
4. He is from Perth and <u>i</u> am from Cardiff.
5. Rich and Ava went to <u>paris</u> in August.
6. Jamie is going to Germany on <u>thursday</u>.
7. Fran and <u>megan</u> are going surfing in Cornwall.

Week 4 — Day 5

1.
2.
3.
4.
5.

Week 5 — Day 1

1. I saw Ewan **when** I was playing outside.
2. Tia put her coat on **when** it started to rain.
3. Look at **what** my dog is doing!
4. Yusif likes it **when** it rains.
5. **What** is that splashing sound?
6. **When** will it be sunny again?
7. She asked **what** my dog is called.
8. **What** a bright umbrella she has!

Week 5 — Day 2

1. Who is reading my book?
2. I forgot where I put the blocks.
3. Who are you playing with?
4. He is the boy who has blue shorts.
5. This is Mina, who I met today.
6. Where should I put the game?

Week 5 — Day 3

1. Do they have robes on?
2. He has leaves in his hair.
3. What is he holding?
4. It is a very hot day.
5. Where is that big boat going?
6. What is that statue made from?
7. He is holding a torch.

Week 5 — Day 4

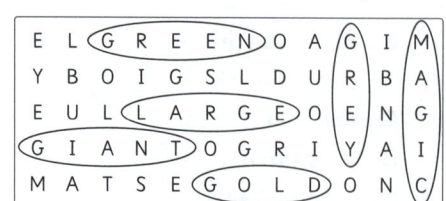

Week 5 — Day 5

1. I am called Roger.
2. I live on Park Road.
3. I live with my mum and my little sister.
4. I love swimming.
5. I have one goat.

Week 6 — Day 1

1. Dev walk**s** to the park.
2. Zoe whizz**es** past us.
3. The bus splash**es** through the rain.
4. We left our lunch**es** in the car.
5. Lucy and I rode our scooter**s**.
6. She catch**es** the train.
7. My dad drive**s** to work.
8. We go to school on our bike**s**.

Week 6 — Day 2

1. yes
2. no
3. yes
4. yes
5. no
6. no

Week 6 — Day 3

1. I eat so much fruit
2. How yummy this is
3. I lost my lemon
4. The fruit can talk
5. That melon is huge
6. The peach has eyes
7. What a strange apple
8. Bananas are so nice

Week 6 — Day 4

1. My **little** brother likes the sand.
2. I found **one** crab.
3. We have **one** beach ball.
4. Emma put a **little** flag on top.
5. The pink **one** is mine.
6. I saw some **little** fish.
7. There is **one** chair left.

Week 6 — Day 5

1.
2. a bow and arrow
3. One mark for each part of the castle that matches the description.

Week 7 — Day 1

1. yes
2. yes
3. no
4. yes
5. no
6. yes
7. no

Week 7 — Day 2

1. We listen**ed** to the music.
2. Nasim wants to be a sing**er**.
3. She loves learn**ing** the keyboard.
4. He is our music teach**er**.
5. They start**ed** to sing.
6. Play**ing** the flute is such fun.
7. Are you go**ing** to the show?
8. Ruby clean**ed** her trumpet.

Week 7 — Day 3

1. Their names are <u>rory</u> and Daisy.
2. <u>my</u> sister Anna says the puppies are clever<u>.</u>
3. Anna and <u>i</u> saw Rory juggling five balls<u>.</u>
4. I showed <u>daisy</u> how to read.
5. My brother <u>joe</u> took the puppies on a plane<u>.</u>
6. <u>now</u> they want to learn how to fly.

Week 7 — Day 4

1. untied
2. unsure
3. helpful
4. unkind
5. caring
6. unsteady
7. unpack
8. afraid

Week 7 — Day 5

1. Nicholas
2. Amy
3. Mrs Sims
4. tidy his desk

Week 8 — Day 1

1. Auntie Evie lets us splash around in our **wellies**.
2. Auntie Ellie **cries** at films.
3. Auntie Rosie reads me **stories**.
4. Auntie Amie loves **fried** eggs.
5. I help Auntie Jennie make **jellies**.
6. Auntie Zadie grows **strawberries**.

Week 8 — Day 2

1. I help my dad **do** the cooking.
2. Archie sorts **out** the clothes.
3. My older brother can **do** the ironing.
4. Milo and Dad go **out** with the dog every day.
5. Mum and I **do** some dusting.
6. She puts the rubbish **out**.
7. We help with the **chores**.

Week 8 — Day 3

1. Is that your kite**?**
2. They are friends**.**
3. What do you eat**?**
4. Why are you pink**?**
5. I like those flowers**.**
6. Where is your hat**?**
7. He has yellow boots**.**
8. She looks cosy**.**

Week 8 — Day 4

1. Avni has a pencil **and** I have a pen.
2. I like maths **and** you like science.
3. Max **and** Leni love school.
4. My bag is blue **and** green.
5. Our teacher is kind **and** funny.
6. We line up **and** wait for lunch.
7. He is painting **and** she is reading.
8. Ella carries the paper **and** the glue.

Week 8 — Day 5

1.
2. brownies and cookies
   (1 mark for each)
3. cherries and blackberries
   (1 mark for each)

Week 9 — Day 1

1.
2.
3.
4.
5.
6.
7.

Week 9 — Day 2

1. I **drive** to the house.
2. He is very **brave**.
3. They **arrive** in time.
4. Please **save** my cat.
5. I **wave** at her.
6. We wear thick **gloves**.
7. I **leave** when it is over.
8. He is **above** me.

Week 9 — Day 3

1. looks after Ivan bats
   2 3 1 4
2. finds bats Jay some
   2 4 1 3
3. caves Tanya the visits
   4 1 3 2
4. Ruth up dressing likes
   1 4 3 2
5. bats chase Pablo the
   2 3 4 1

Week 9 — Day 4

1. Jen has a pink hair clip.
2. Santino and I like to smile.
3. My hair is long and curly.
4. Lia looks a lot like Tess.
5. He has a light blue shirt.
6. Ally wears a gold necklace.
7. Yusra is taller than I am.

Week 9 — Day 5
1. a surfboard
2. at the beach
3. Any sensible drawing.

Week 10 — Day 1
1. Milly put **some** sunglasses in her bag.
2. Luca would **like** to bring his book.
3. My teddy will **come** with me.
4. We need **some** towels.
5. I **like** to take crayons with me.
6. We will pack **some** socks.
7. Please can you **come** and help me carry it?

Week 10 — Day 2
1. Nico
2. Ian
3. Tom
4. Kath
5. Hans

Week 10 — Day 3
1. Oliver walk**ed** onto the stage.
2. Read**ing** lines is really fun.
3. Andy play**ed** a cheeky puppy.
4. Ling turn**ed** up on time.
5. Alba is the loudest speak**er**.
6. Ron miss**ed** the show.
7. My friends are very good at sing**ing**.
8. Bella dress**ed** as a cat.

Week 10 — Day 4
1. Where can I get a map?
2. Thank you for helping me!
3. Should I turn left or right?
4. Which way is the fastest?
5. That was such a long road!
6. I have found the zoo at last!

Week 10 — Day 5
1.
2. a cat / a silver cat
3. nice
4. He has to eat every bit of his dinner.

Week 11 — Day 1
1. We **were** ready to make a snowman.
2. My friend Peter was **there** too.
3. Our snowmen **were** so big.
4. Look at that one over **there**!
5. Are **there** any carrots left?
6. The arms **were** made from sticks.
7. **There** are the buttons we used for eyes.
8. I thought they **were** never going to melt.

Week 11 — Day 2
1. no
2. yes
3. no
4. yes
5. no
6. yes

Week 11 — Day 3
1. My little **cousin** Leo came with me.
2. Can **you** jump high?
3. A **group** of children joined in with us.
4. We **could** touch the top.
5. I **counted** how many times I jumped.
6. My **shoulders** were hurting.
7. We ran **around** to the slide.

Week 11 — Day 4
1. Robert smiles very widely.
2. Elsa has two toothbrushes.
3. Marco is a dentist.
4. Penny lost her tooth.

Week 11 — Day 5
1. cloud
2. a storm
3. Taj's tummy

Week 12 — Day 1
1. My **family** were excited to see the castle.
2. We waited **by** the gate.
3. You had to show **your** ticket.
4. It was **very** busy inside.
5. There were **many** things to see.
6. I bought **myself** a gift from the shop.
7. I am glad the weather was **dry**.

Week 12 — Day 2
1. We went **out** to look for butterflies.
2. Jerry saw a pink **one** by the tree.
3. There were some **little** butterflies in the field.
4. **One** landed on my head.
5. It had **little** stripes on its wings.
6. I asked Jerry what I should **do**.
7. I helped it get **out** of my hair.
8. **Do** you like butterflies?

Week 12 — Day 3
1. Mum came back with a huge ice cream. — 3
2. I was very upset and nearly cried. — 5
3. Oh no! I dropped it on the ground! — 4
4. Mum went to buy me a yummy treat. — 1
5. I sat on a bench and waited for her. — 2

Week 12 — Day 4
1. **When** will our room be ready?
2. **What** floor is our room on?
3. **What** is our room number?
4. **When** is breakfast served?
5. **When** do the shops open?
6. **What** is on the dinner menu?
7. **What** has the weather been like?
8. **When** do we have to leave the hotel?

Week 12 — Day 5
1.
2. stick
3. wood
4. fingers